101

ORIGINAL PRAYER QUOTES

VOL. 1

Daniel de Eagle

eBook ISBN: 978-969-3992-76-2

PAPERBACK ISBN: 978-969-3992-77-9

HARDBACK ISBN: 978-969-3992-78-6

Library of Congress Control Number: 2015904837

Daniel de Eagle, Euless , TX

Table of Content

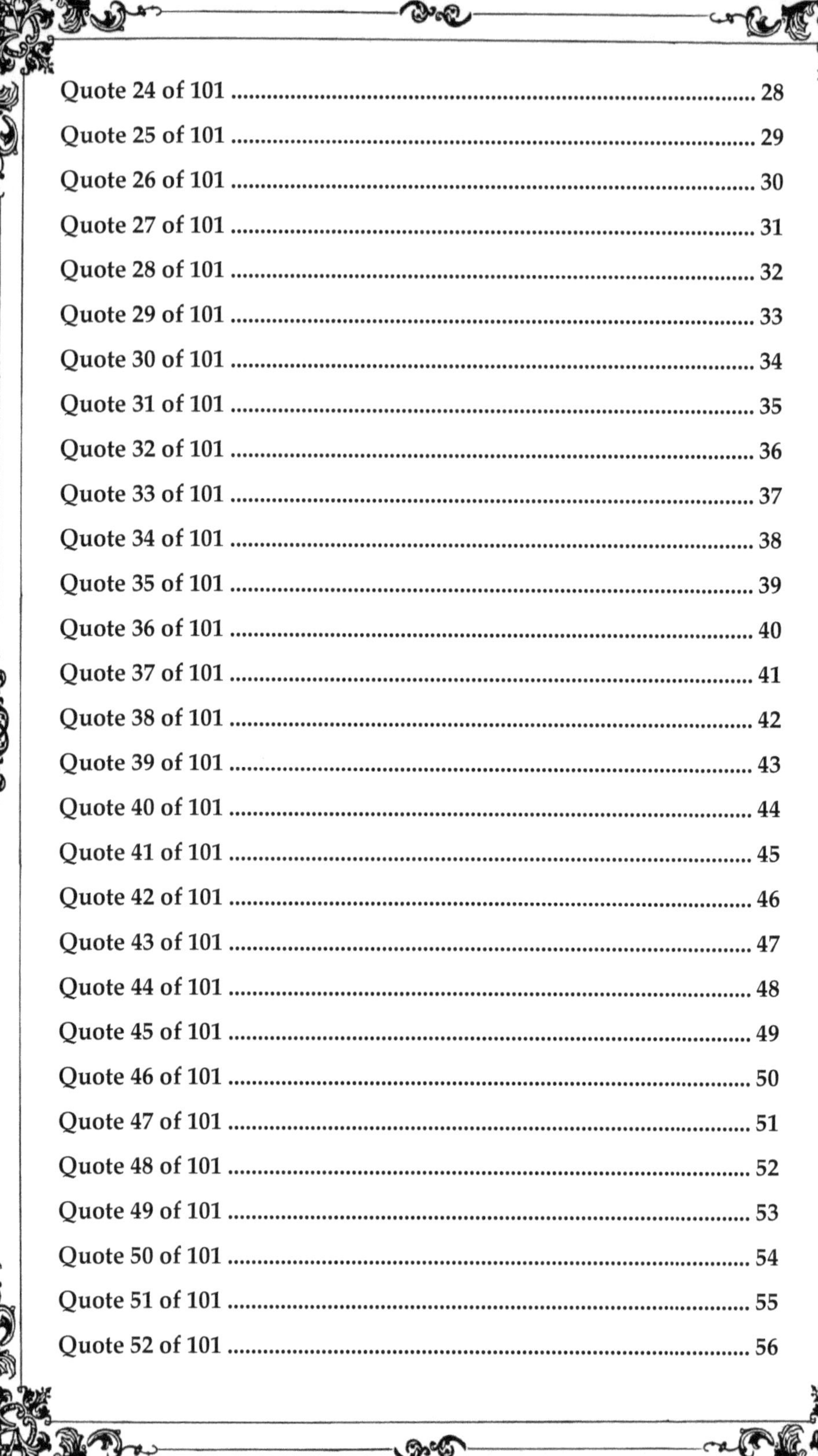

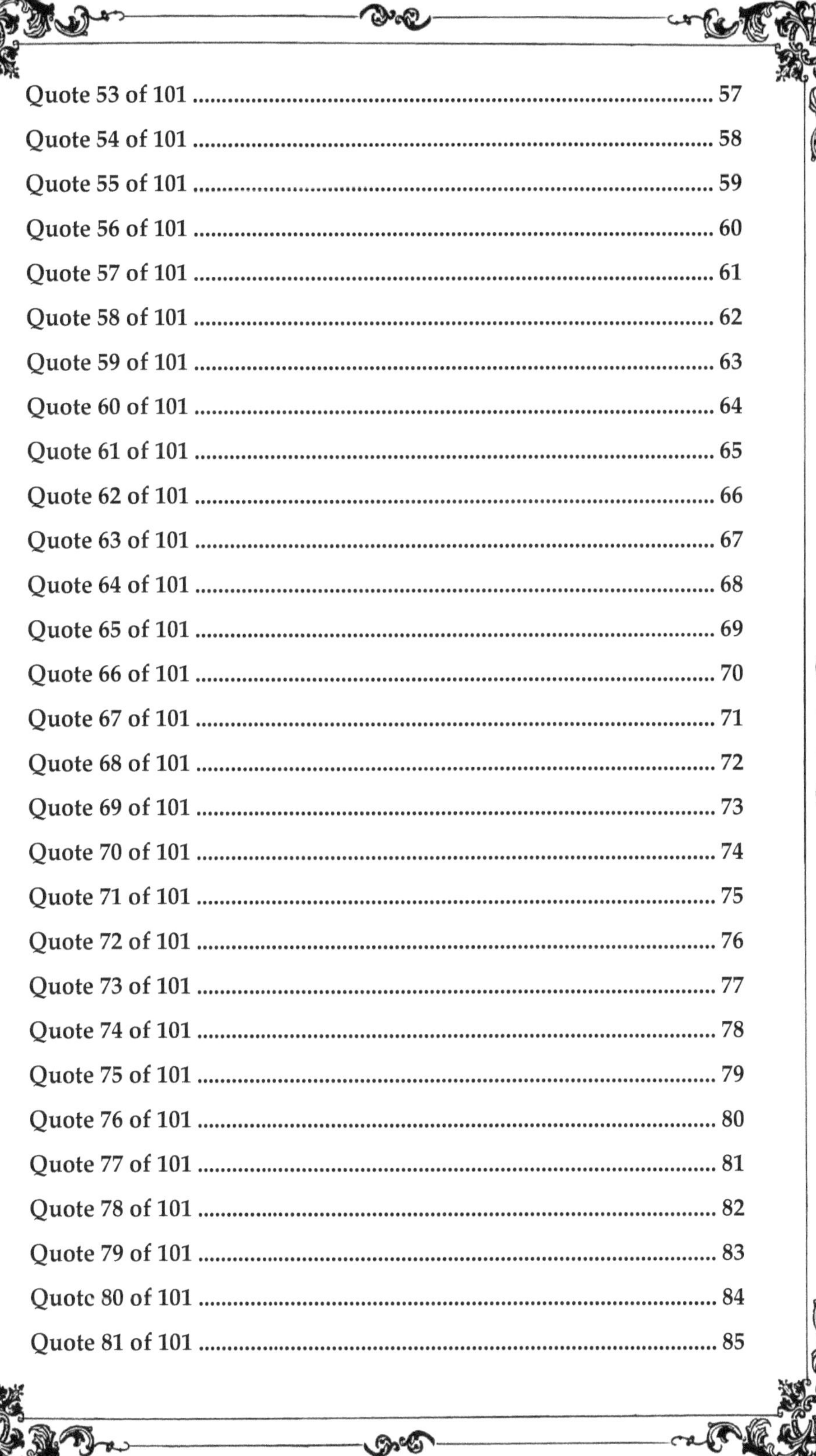

Dedication

To all those who seek meaning and introspection in the journey of life, "101 Original Prayer Quotes Vol.1" is dedicated to you. In these pages, I hope to offer a collection of prayer quotes and reflections that resonate with your soul, providing guidance, comfort, and inspiration as you navigate life's twists and turns. May these original prayer quotes serve as a source of wisdom and passion, connecting with both the present generation and those who will follow, carrying timeless lessons and heartfelt sentiments for all who seek them.

As we journey through the tapestry of life, may these prayer quotes serve as a reminder of the enduring power of faith, hope, and love. It is my sincere wish that these words resonate with your heart, offering solace and encouragement in moments of doubt and celebration in moments of joy. With each prayer quote, may you find a renewed sense of purpose and a deepened connection to the Creator and Father of all, guiding you through life's lessons and inspiring the generations to come.

To the seekers of truth, the dreamers of dreams, and the believers in the power of prayer, this book is dedicated to you. May these original prayer quotes ignite a passion for life's lessons and serve as a timeless beacon of hope for all who turn its pages.

About Daniel de Eagle

Daniel de Eagle is a dedicated servant leader and prayer missionary from the Generation X timeline. He serves as the co-ministry leader of Covering Eagle Ministries alongside Minister Nikki his spouse. Daniel also serves as Lead Prayer Strategist and Trainer at When Eagles Pray Trainer (W.E.P.T.), an arm of CEM that provides strategic online and in-person prayer resources to the local and global Body of Christ.

With a remarkable 39 years of active involvement in the prayer ministry, Daniel is known for his strong flow in prophetic intercession and his ability to offer deep yet simplistic teaching insights on all aspects of prayer, catering to individuals at various levels of Christian maturity. He firmly believes that prayer is from the heart and about producing tangible results, as inspired by James 5:16.

Throughout his journey, Daniel has served on the leadership teams of numerous church-led and ancillary ministry-led prayer initiatives across Europe, Africa, and North America. He currently serves as a Governmental Level Intercessor for certain nations while personally providing prayer coverage to global Church Leaders.

Daniel's passions extend to marriage and family, prayer, and the marketplace. In 1997, he completed his Diploma in Christian Ministries program with a focus on Youth and Community development at CICM, UK. Additionally, he holds an Associate Degree in International Business and Trade, as well as a Bachelor's degree in Business Administration with a specialization in Small Business Management.

For the past 26 years, Daniel has been happily married to his wife and ministry partner, Nikki. Together, they cohost the annual Marriage Reignited Gala event, which celebrates and strengthens the marriages of heterosexual couples.

To connect with Daniel and stay updated on his work, you can follow him on Twitter @daniel_de_eagle, Instagram as daniel_de_eagle, find his YouTube channel under the name Daniel de Eagle, and locate him on Facebook as Daniel de Eagle. His inspirational quotes can also be found on the Facebook Page "Prayer Quotes and Reflections". He can also be found on TikTok under the username @daniel_de_eagle.

In the words of Daniel himself, "I'm not esoteric but I spit lyrics as a timeless psychedelic cleric on the Word hallucinogenic with a unique homiletic style." This quote captures the essence of his personality and resonates with present-day and tech-savvy generations.

About the book

"101 Original Prayer Quotes" by Daniel de Eagle is a heartfelt collection of prayer quotes and reflections that offer guidance, comfort, and inspiration for those navigating life's journey. With timeless wisdom and heartfelt sentiments, these original prayer quotes resonate with seekers of truth, dreamers of dreams, and believers in the power of prayer. This book serves as a beacon of hope, igniting a passion for life's lessons and connecting with both present and future generations.

As we journey through the tapestry of life, may these prayer quotes serve as a reminder of the enduring power of faith, hope, and love. It is the author's sincere wish that these words resonate with your heart, offering solace and encouragement in moments of doubt and celebration in moments of joy. With each prayer quote, may you find a renewed sense of purpose and a deepened connection to the Creator and Father of all, guiding you through life's lessons and inspiring the generations to come.

To the seekers of truth, the dreamers of dreams, and the believers in the power of prayer, this book is dedicated to you. May these original prayer quotes ignite a passion for life's lessons and serve as a timeless beacon of hope for all who turn its pages.

Developing an internal prayer perseverance system enables you to bounce back instead of remaining defeated when faced with the unpredictable challenges of life.

~ Daniel de Eagle

Remember to find your balance with prayer, as it unveils the unseen and empowers you to bring about meaningful transformations in your reality and time here on earth.

~ Daniel de Eagle

When we pray, we do not play. When the world sees us pray, they think it's a play. When they see God results, they just got played.

~ Daniel de Eagle

When we make a habit of praying ahead of time, we severely limit the chances of straying in time. Watch and Pray.

~ Daniel de Eagle

Individuals following the command to love your neighbor as you love yourself also entail knowing and praying for your local neighborhood, province, city, and state.

~ Daniel de Eagle

Stay prayerful, for life's blows and challenges only make you shine as a testimony. Stay aglow.

~ Daniel de Eagle

Life is a series of decisions laced with opportunities for getting closer to God. If I let myself get spaced out, I won't be able to benefit humanity.

~ Daniel de Eagle

Establish a prayer foundation for your bloodline today, so that when any adversary, player or the slayer comes, the family will be supernaturally protected.

~ Daniel de Eagle

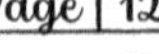

Embedded in prayers that God answers is a declaration of dependence. Asking, seeking, and knocking are rooted in approaching boldly through the blood of Jesus.

~ Daniel de Eagle

Quality personal prayer time positions me to publicly testify about remarkable and bazaar prayer results, not bizarre or unusual ones. Make time to pray.

~ Daniel de Eagle

To walk in God's will and juice, you can't afford to cruise, or you'll get bruised. To be like Nicky Cruz in your generation, then immerse yourself in and fully embrace God's Word and prayer.

~ Daniel de Eagle

Respect the warfare. Inspect your armory. Expect the Holy Spirit every time. The context of living is your call. The contest for God's anointing demands your whole being's sharpness in His Word and prayer.

~ Daniel de Eagle

Though you're sane, if my pain you can't feel, How can you pray me back from the enemy's chain to my domain where I may reign especially In a situation not easily fixed?

~ Daniel de Eagle

God flock if you forget the Father, you'll knock in prayer and get zilch, and sulk. God demands your mindedness of Him as Rock of all ages.

~ Daniel de Eagle

When on a God-glorifying assignment and you pray again, God dazzles the senses while you whoop the situation till it fizzles out.

~ Daniel de Eagle

My heart stays guarded by God's Word, and I stay prayed up while remaining hyped up on my hope in God and on God's love for me.

~ Daniel de Eagle

Youths and young adults, the challenges and devils you face are permitted by God to take you to higher levels as you pray and overcome. Defeating evil powers gets you to your progressive towers.

~ Daniel de Eagle

When you're fired up in the Word and prayer, the worm, germ, squirm, and fake perm in lukewarm Christianity let go of you so the Luke in you can arise to become a living epistle read by everyone.

~ Daniel de Eagle

Don't get it twisted, prayer is a discipline, not a crutch. Prayer helps build inner fortitude to face times in solitude and with the multitude.

~ Daniel de Eagle

Quote 20 of 101

Praying folks, it's important that we learn to go to the throne of grace before we go to the phone of gossip and slander.

~ Daniel de Eagle

Know that we're all prone to unleash a mouth drone, so moan alone before God. Dethrone self. Don't let the situation be overblown or overgrown with weeds.

~ Daniel de Eagle

Children routinely pray at night before you lay down, and also pray during the day before you go to play with your clay.

~ Daniel de Eagle

Quote 23 of 101

As we grow older and grey, we pray so our play doesn't lead us astray but fortifies us to stay and display His glory.

~ Daniel de Eagle

If you've been facing an issue for a long while with no changes and you don't want to be stuck as a dumbo, then a combo of prayer and fasting might be needed as a powerful jumbo solution.

~ Daniel de Eagle

A complete encounter with the Word isn't just when we read and feed on the Word alone. To prayerfully intercede is the deed we need to add to heal our world.

~ Daniel de Eagle

It's not enough to pray. When I stray, I betray the ones I love and set myself up as prey. Woe betides me if I fail to live life as a protégé.

~ Daniel de Eagle

A lion and a cat both having feline DNA doesn't mean they exert the same influence. We're all Christians doesn't mean we all obey and pray the same.

~ Daniel de Eagle

When I awoke today, I needed to soak in prayers, so I spoke with God and received smoke from the horns of God's altar. Thereafter, I stopped feeling spiritually broke.

~ Daniel de Eagle

To ask in prayer outside the manifest presence of God is like trying to task with a mask on. Be wise, so ask while you bask in the presence of God.

~ Daniel de Eagle

Quote 30 of 101

I live to pray, becoming a live wire, and pray to live. When I leave, those I trained will relieve me of this prayer drive, and I assure you, they will strive farther and further than I did.

~ Daniel de Eagle

Prayer isn't just for us to unload and dump on God. Remember, God wants to infuse and pump His life into us as well. It takes two to tango, so don't be the pet called Bingo when praying.

~ Daniel de Eagle

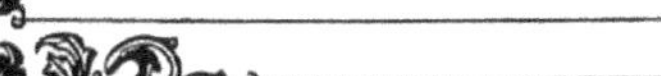

Quote 32 of 101

It's concerning to think that we're praying only 1 or 2 days out of 7 and expecting the thickening presence of God to bring an unprecedented awakening in our timeline and generation.

~ Daniel de Eagle

Quote 33 of 101

The Prayer Diary is for today. You get to journal and pray in your prayer diary. The enemy gets played while Jesus has the final say and day.

~ Daniel de Eagle

Quote 34 of 101

The ultimate lesson from the Apex Navy seal is that being a Prayer seal involves missing a meal, honing a biblically renewed mind of steel, and always being willing to kneel.

~ Daniel de Eagle

On this side of eternity, we groan in pain and prayer for the loss of those dear to our hearts, but as long as Emmanuel is on the throne, we are not alone.

~ Daniel de Eagle

Before I can pray outside, I first have to pray inside. Before I can take the east side or the west side, I have to first take care of my soul side.

~ Daniel de Eagle

Praying is not a game. It doesn't lead to fame on its own, but it will keep you from shame in any arena. To say you can't pray is pretty lame and limiting.

~ Daniel de Eagle

Quote 38 of 101

No one has a special claim to an extraordinary prayer life. If there's a storm in your life, tame it with fervent prayer until you weaken and maim it significantly.

~ Daniel de Eagle

If enemies bring a lawful claim for my captivity via past shame, I counterclaim in prayer through Jesus Christ, who became a curse so that I might receive Abraham's blessings.

~ Daniel de Eagle

If any situation or anyone tries to give you a negative name that's not yours, then rename yourself in the place of prayer with God's Word.

~ Daniel de Eagle

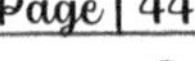

When coming to God in prayer, there is an exchange. So why settle for ABC when God imparts the alpha, the in-between, and the omega of the matter?

~ Daniel de Eagle

From now on, when you encounter the "All Knowing One," make sure you come out of the prayer encounter with solutions, not just tidbits or goosebumps.

~ Daniel de Eagle

Quote 43 of 101

Grateful for hope that's dope enough to cope in the here and now, absent of any horoscope, but also has the audacity to envelope our eternity when we pray and stay in the Word.

~ Daniel de Eagle

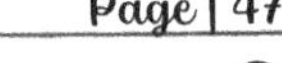

Pray up a storm to stay in top form. Failing to pray will make you lukewarm. Read the Word, and God will transform your mind. To perform in any field, stay informed by His Word.

~ Daniel de Eagle

Why do we pray? We pray so we don't become the prey, so delay won't be denial, so we don't easily stray. We pray so we don't disobey by neglecting to pray.

~ Daniel de Eagle

Read the Word and pray early. Life is a play, and you're the actor. Take your role seriously. The box office payoff that will be yours is immense when you daily rehearse your part in prayer.

~ Daniel de Eagle

To pray is to slay in defeat my demons' influence. If I stray a lot, the contract is renewed, and he brings seven stronger ones to disrupt my life even more.

~ Daniel de Eagle

Learn to lay before God as you pray. Obey God's Word, and you'll hear Heaven's approval with a full tray. Don't let the enemy or what's visible sway you.

~ Daniel de Eagle

Pray through the storms to stay in form. Fail to pray and be lukewarm. Read the Word, and God will transform your mind. To perform in any field, stay informed.

~ Daniel de Eagle

Quote 50 of 101

Cares and scares can make our hairs stand, but prayers with tears to God, who hears and bears us up, keep us going on with fewer fears.

~ Daniel de Eagle

My direction in life is based on my internal wiring. If I feel like I'm losing motivation, perhaps I might need God's inspiring Word and prayer to change my seeing and hearing.

~ Daniel de Eagle

Portraying or posturing to pray is no substitute for actually praying. To be found staying and obeying without decaying, let's continue paying the price on our knees in prayer.

~ Daniel de Eagle

Quote 53 of 101

Through Jesus' bloodline, prayer opens Heaven's chatline and brings you to the Father's frontline. Stay in line despite any jawline challenges, and you'll reach the finish line.

~ Daniel de Eagle

Quote 54 of 101

Many try to make us cry, but praying the Word has taken us beyond the sky to the Most High. We now apply ourselves like a samurai to achieve our goals.

~ Daniel de Eagle

It's illegal for an eagle to take permission from a seagull to soar with regal grace, just as it's essential for us to pray in time with time.

~ Daniel de Eagle

The hurricane doesn't hold a campaign with any airplane to gain domain on whom should first show restraint. Now regain yourself, overcome with prayer and God's Word.

~ Daniel de Eagle

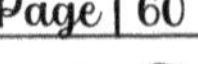

Rome wasn't built overnight, and likewise, a home or business will not bloom without prayer and hard work fueled by determination.

~ Daniel de Eagle

Prayer, in a sense, is giving voice to the soul's longings. Poise hinged on praise of Adonai precedes the focused chase in prayer.

~ Daniel de Eagle

Prayer and a biblical melody flowing through your soul keep you from being tardy while allowing you to enjoy Heaven's rhapsody.

~ Daniel de Eagle

Maintain an appetite for God through delighting in His Word. Invite His presence through prayer. His oversight negates fright and makes your efforts tight.

~ Daniel de Eagle

In the light of a new day, it's alright to ignite our day with thanks and prayer to the One who gave us sight to behold another opportunity.

~ Daniel de Eagle

Life is a stage. The "how to" determines whether you engage or become a voiceless bystander in life. Prayer is a multi-stage juice for any page life serves you.

~ Daniel de Eagle

Quote 63 of 101

Let passion rise within you and wage war in prayer against anything trying to deter you from the mandate to step onto your stage as you go and make disciples for Christ.

~ Daniel de Eagle

My mentor Dr. Tayo Adeyemi was a prayer warrior and priest. He turned me into one through intense prayer sessions and deep immersion in the Word, and now I remain a fruitful follower.

~ Daniel de Eagle

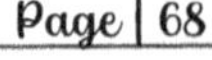

When you pray, do all you can to ensure God is at the center of your turbulence or praise avalanche as you continue to find your footing.

~ Daniel de Eagle

After you've prayed and feel that you have the victory, know that the next step is to work it out in the natural based on the insights received.

~ Daniel de Eagle

Soaking in prayers is the recipe for openly invoking God's presence. Publicly, you'll be stoking Heaven's fire while revoking evil's influence.

~ Daniel de Eagle

"Wow, to God!" That's the impact you'll have in public when you consistently make a habit of praying in private before you pray in public.

~ Daniel de Eagle

Quote 69 of 101

Prayer is an adventure, with God's Word as the map for the journey, His presence ensuring you're on the right path, and the Holy Spirit providing the necessary strength to persevere.

~ Daniel de Eagle

When you pray a storm, we may think you're a bum on rum but when we hear your drum roll of victory and success, we'll know you're from Jesus.

~ Daniel de Eagle

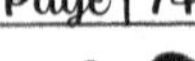

Collaborative prayers across the globe is the carriage that gives passage to the greatest revival, transforming it from a mirage to a barrage.

~ Daniel de Eagle

For the awakening to occur, there must be a purposeful and collective effort to kindle the fires of revival through prayer across the globe.

~ Daniel de Eagle

Revival will only be talk and illusion until a significant number of people across the global divide individually step up in prayer.

~ Daniel de Eagle

My prayers can make or break me. I would rather be made so I chose to pray all manner of prayers.

~ Daniel de Eagle

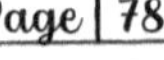

We are God's deputies on earth, changing the atmosphere when we pray. Right things happen when someone prays.

~ Daniel de Eagle

God honors quality time spent in prayer, regardless of who you are.

~ Daniel de Eagle

Christians don't instinctively know how to pray. Church and Christian interactions must foster a culture that promotes prayer.

~ Daniel de Eagle

Quote 78 of 101

A praying culture ensures that the resurrection life flowing through us is spent in service, not leaking without purpose.

~ Daniel de Eagle

Quote 79 of 101

Lord, you saw me fall and endure my hell. I prayed, and you rescued me with a call of hallelujah.

~ Daniel de Eagle

Approach praying with a long-term investor's mindset, shaping tomorrow with today's actions.

~ Daniel de Eagle

When you pray, you become a storm brewer, leaving behind unshakable stuff! #StormBrewers.

~ Daniel de Eagle

A global prayer mindset in all churches ensures we don't warm ourselves with campfires in the face of snowstorms.

~ Daniel de Eagle

Pray forward for the next generation. You're here today because someone prayed to birth you into faith. #PrayItForward.

~ Daniel de Eagle

Pray! God hears without delay. Use the time between your cry's relay to the throne of Grace to replay God's Word in your mind and speech.

~ Daniel de Eagle

Quote 85 of 101

Individuals ignite campfires, but together we unleash a global storm. Let's elevate our prayers to a global level. #GlobalPrayer.

~ Daniel de Eagle

Quote 86 of 101

Intolerance binds us, rejecting indifference. Embrace intolerance of prayerlessness.

~ Daniel de Eagle

After all is said and done, we pray to uncover our true selves and chart our course. Discovering purpose and direction is essential.

~ Daniel de Eagle

Embrace change, it's the hallmark of your years to come. Don't think it strange that prayer will be crucial as you arrange, rearrange, and exchange in your life.

~ Daniel de Eagle

Quote 89 of 101

Pray more, don't betray the Jesus mandate. Start with your neighborhood, pray life into homes.

~ Daniel de Eagle

Prayer is Heaven's essence, keeping us glowing, showing Jesus Christ in our hustle. Keep growing, whether it's snowing or the sun's shining.

~ Daniel de Eagle

Quote 91 of 101

Entering the place of prayer takes you from the place of "could have", "should have" or "would have" to the place of "now have" by faith.

~ Daniel de Eagle

Quote 92 of 101

Embrace the change within your range, stay prayerful. Exchange the past for the present God has stored for you, even if it seems strange initially.

~ Daniel de Eagle

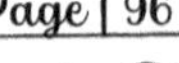

Sitting on a two-legged chair is unsteady unless it's a bench. Prayer requires insight from God's Word, the Holy Spirit, and you.

~ Daniel de Eagle

Continue to pray, for His presence brings gaiety. Some call it insanity, others spew profanity, but in His reality, find serenity.

~ Daniel de Eagle

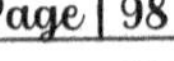

No matter how much you know come as laity in prayer before the Deity of Eternity. An encounter with Him will turn your dubiety to certainty.

~ Daniel de Eagle

Successful prayer depends on insights from God's Word, like a garden needs water and sunlight.

~ Daniel de Eagle

Prayer dampens my crazy sensuality, awakens my spirituality.
Prayer allows my faculty to experience His majesty and pageantry
in my humanity.

~ Daniel de Eagle

With a life of prayer based on God's Word by faith the Bible moves from being a historical book to a living reality experienced daily.

~ Daniel de Eagle

You don't need a soothsayer, doomsayer, naysayer or gainsayer to know that if you don't have a prayer life you'll likely be a self-betrayer.

~ Daniel de Eagle

Quote 100 of 101

Whether you're young or seasoned an intentionality in doing whatever it takes to seek God early through prayer and His Word makes the difference between a meaningful or meaningless life.

~ Daniel de Eagle

Quote 101 of 101

After all is said and done "ongoing obedience to the process" is the price to pay to excel in any craft or gifting. Grow prayer by praying.

~ Daniel de Eagle

www.ingramcontent.com/pod-product-compliance
Lightning Source LLC
Chambersburg PA
CBHW040815120726
48005CB00012B/1421